the Pentecost Story

THE STORY OF THE COMING OF THE HOLY SPIRIT: GENESIS 11:1–9
AND ACTS 2:1–41 FOR CHILDREN

WRITTEN BY ELIZABETH JAEGER

ILLUSTRATED BY DAVE HILL

Long ago in Babylon,

When earth was very young,

The people all lived in one place,

They spoke one common tongue.

They didn't think they needed

God's help or strength at all;

They built themselves a city,

With a tower, tall.

"Our tower touches heaven!"

The people said with glee,

"We're so awesome! We're so cool!

There's nothing we can't be!"

The Lord came down to see it,

The tower that they made,

He said, "I'm so unhappy

To know how far they've strayed.

As long as they're one people

And speak one language too,

There won't be any limits

To what mankind can do!"

"They think that they don't need Me,

They're fine all on their own.

But sin will be their downfall;

They'll get nothing done alone."

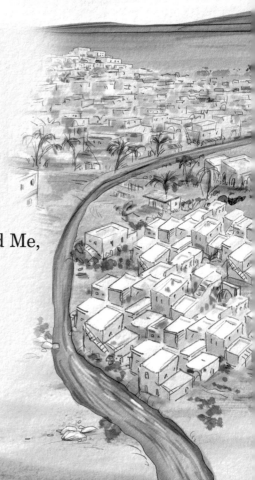

God scattered all the people,

Through every single land,

And mixed up all their languages

So they couldn't understand.

That's why there are many kinds

Of language, color, race.

God spread out all His people

Through every land and place.

Much later, God sent Jesus,

His one and only Son,

To come and save the world from sin,

To make us all be one.

He died and rose to heaven,

And told us that He'd send

The promised Holy Spirit,

Our teacher and our friend.

The followers of Jesus

Were gathered in one place

With folks from everywhere,

From every land and race.

The Holy Spirit blew down,

Like a strong wind He came,

And rested on all Jesus' friends

As tiny tongues of flame.

They all spoke of Jesus' love

So everyone could hear,

Each in his native language,

In words both LOUD and CLEAR.

Three thousand people cried out,

"Oh, Lord, what should we do?"

"Turn back! Be baptized!" Peter said,

"Every one of you!"

The people did what Peter said,

And so the church began.

On that day called "Pentecost"

God's Spirit filled the land.

God sends His Holy Spirit,

And we'll be one in love,

Sent out to tell His story,

God's message from above.

Since the tower of Babel fell,

Our speech is not the same;

On Pentecost, the Spirit

Made us one in Jesus' name.

Dear Parents,

Have you ever heard a parent say to a child, "Use your words"? Sign language aside, gestures go only so far when we're trying to communicate. It is words—written and spoken—that are our best communication tools. This truth was felt by the Babylonians when God destroyed their tower. Without words, they couldn't accomplish their goal, so they abandoned it. Until that time, all of God's people spoke the same language. After that time, the people were divided.

The coming of the Holy Spirit on Pentecost occurred when people were assembled in one place to celebrate the harvest and God's blessing. Part of the feast was an offering of grain and included a ritual that was spoken in Hebrew. The problem was that some people didn't speak or understand Hebrew, so they didn't understand what was said. They didn't hear God's Word.

The fifty days before this had been filled with wonderful but puzzling events: the Lord had suffered and died; but then He rose from the grave, walked and talked among the people, and was bodily lifted into the sky. And now this.

As thousands were worshiping, the sound of the wind was as loud as a tornado. The tongues of fire leaped and danced but didn't burn. Jesus' disciples had the sudden ability to speak languages they'd never spoken before. The people heard the powerful, saving word of forgiveness and salvation through Christ. They understood it. And they believed.

Now, through God the Spirit, the saving Gospel of Jesus Christ is spoken to all people and received.

The Editor